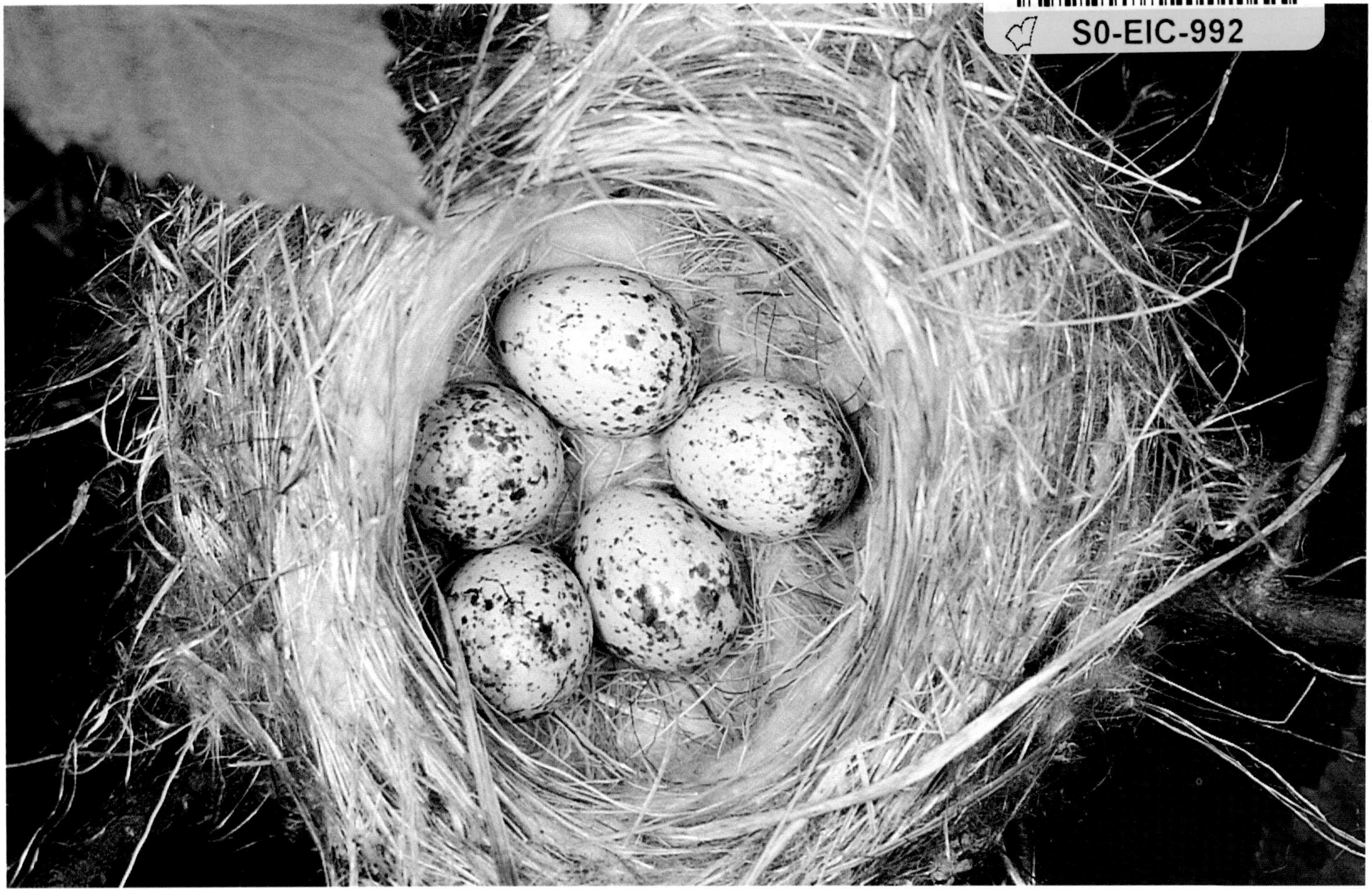

nest

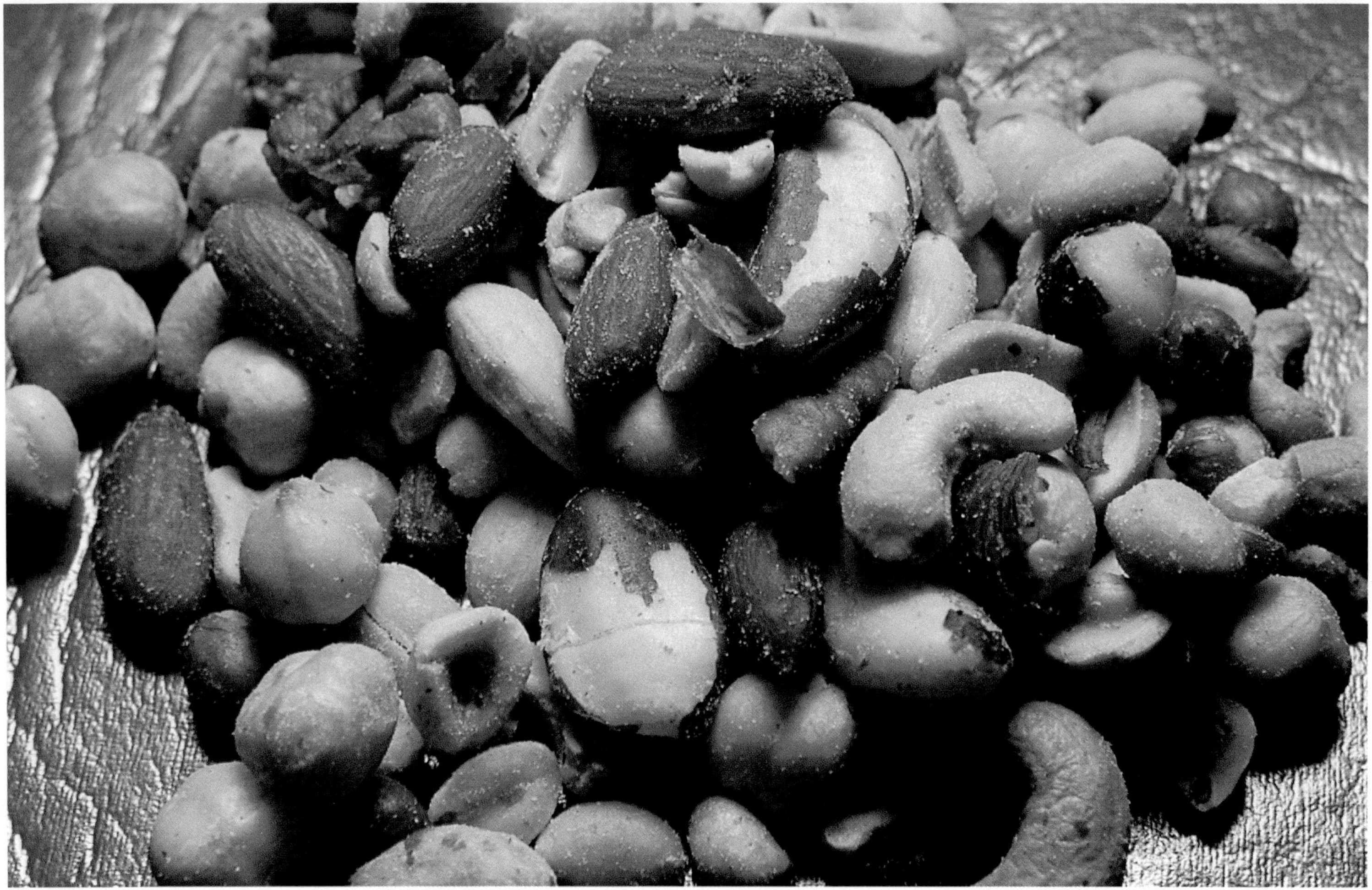

nuts

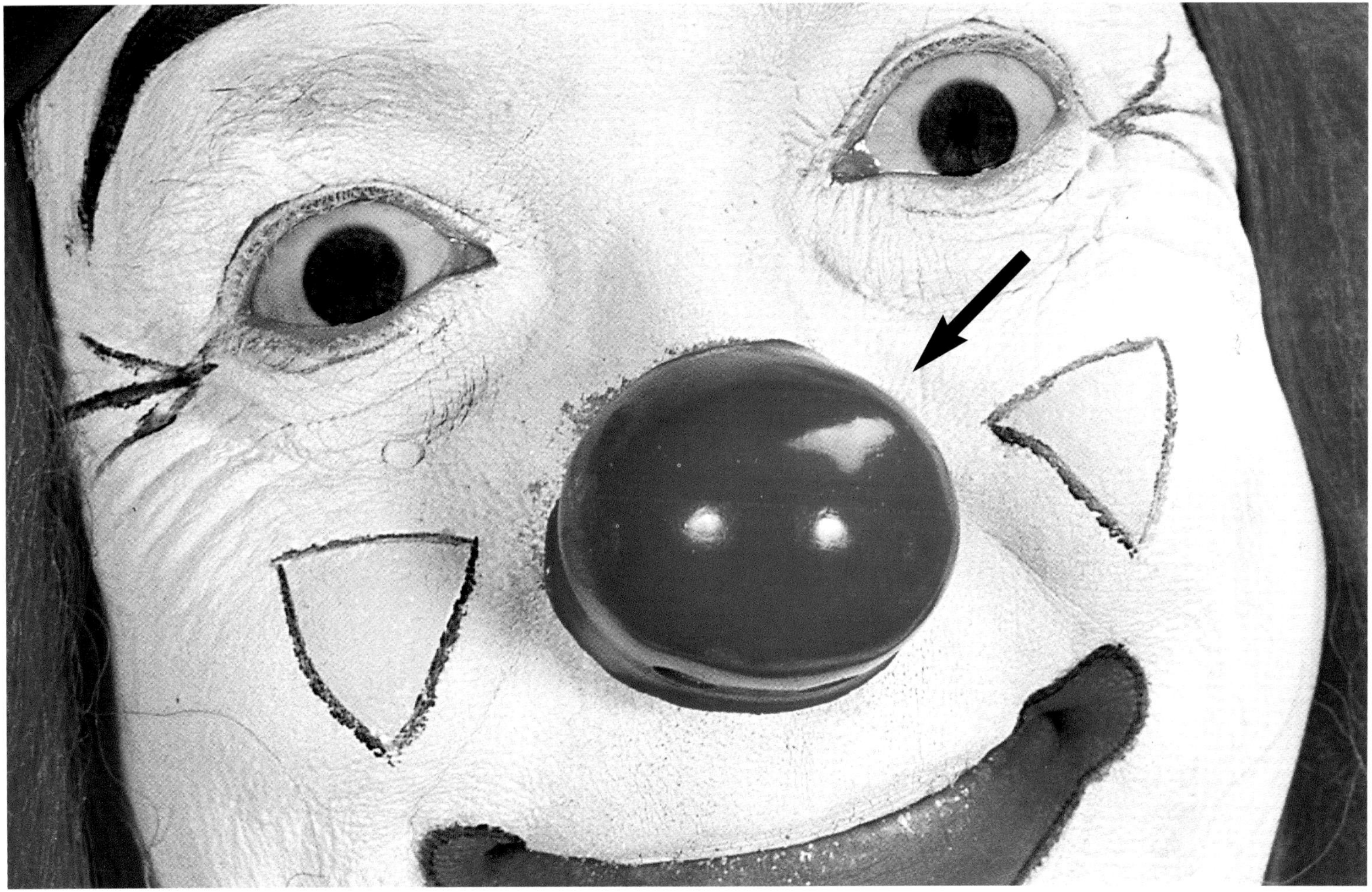

nose

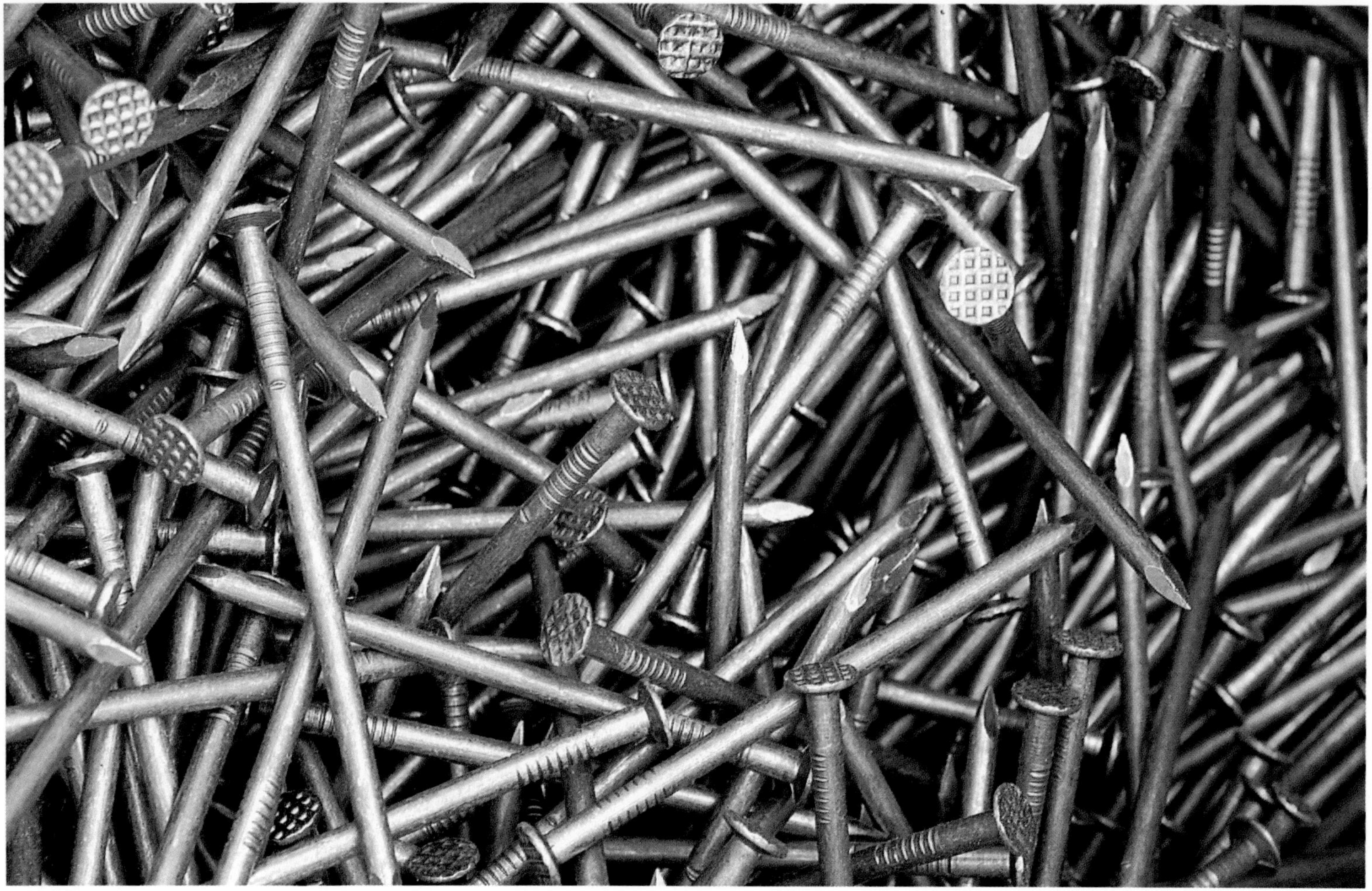

nails

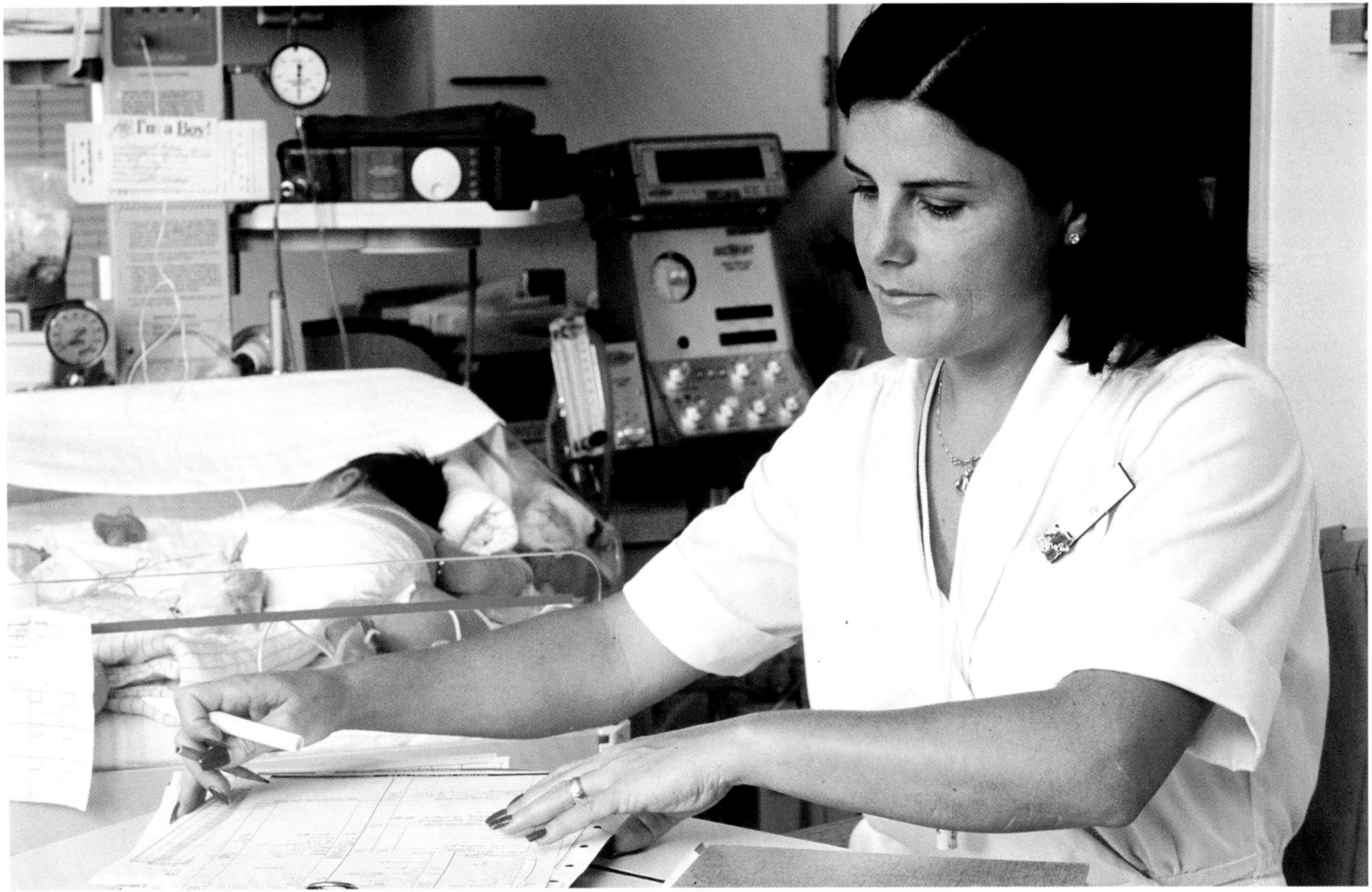

nurse

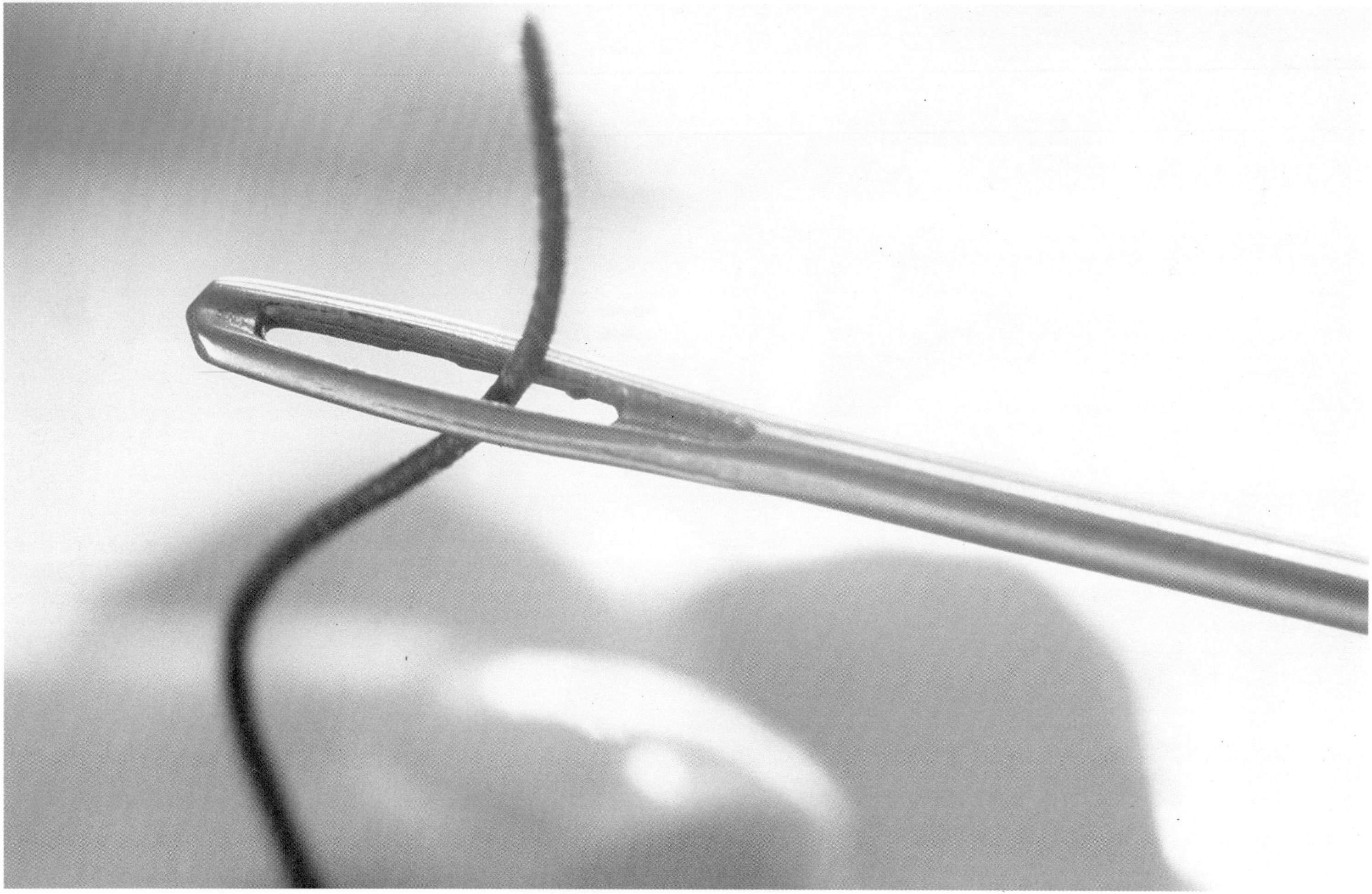

needle

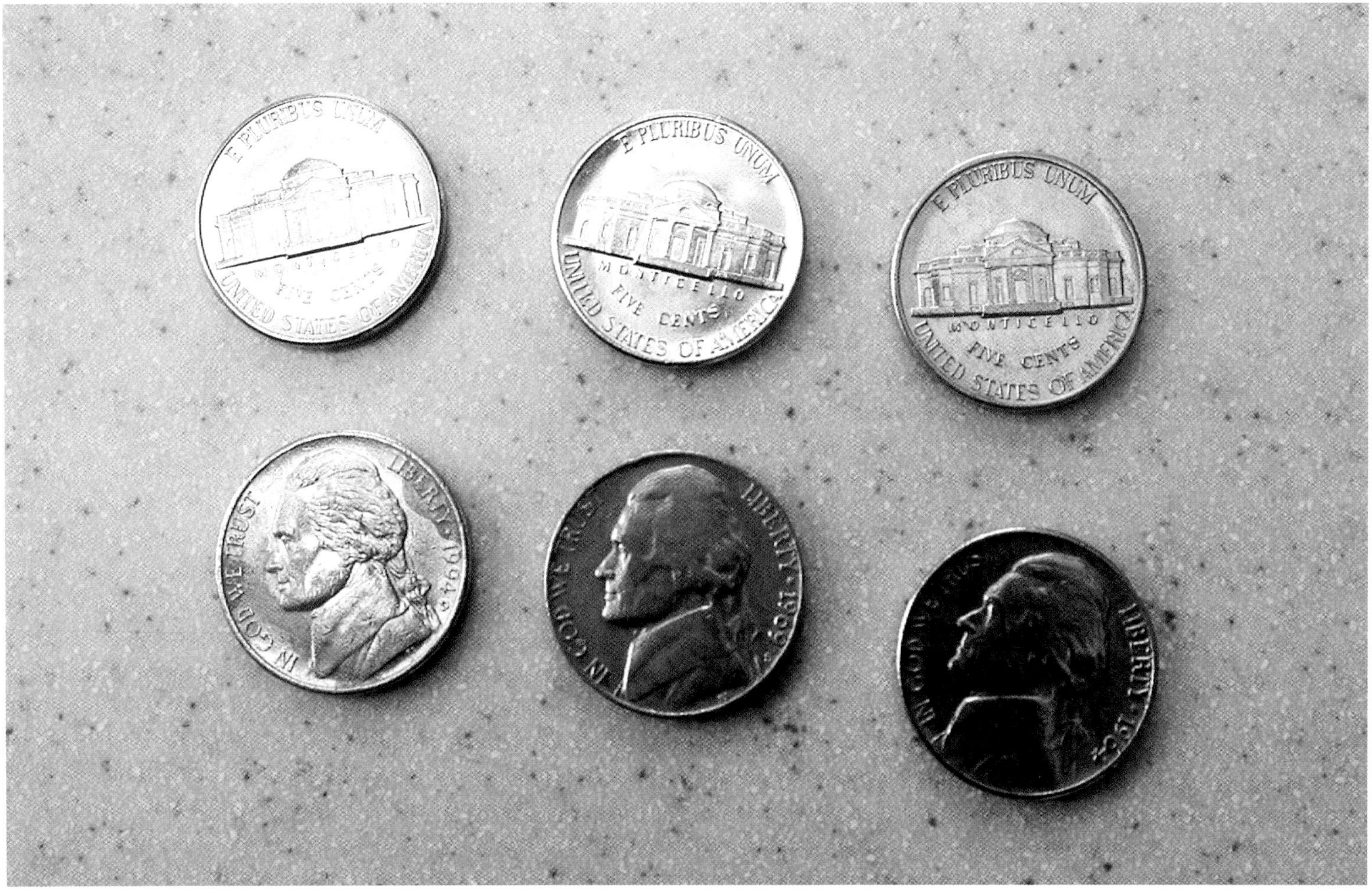
E PLURIBUS UNUM
MONTICELLO
FIVE CENTS
UNITED STATES OF AMERICA
IN GOD WE TRUST
LIBERTY
1994
1969

nickels

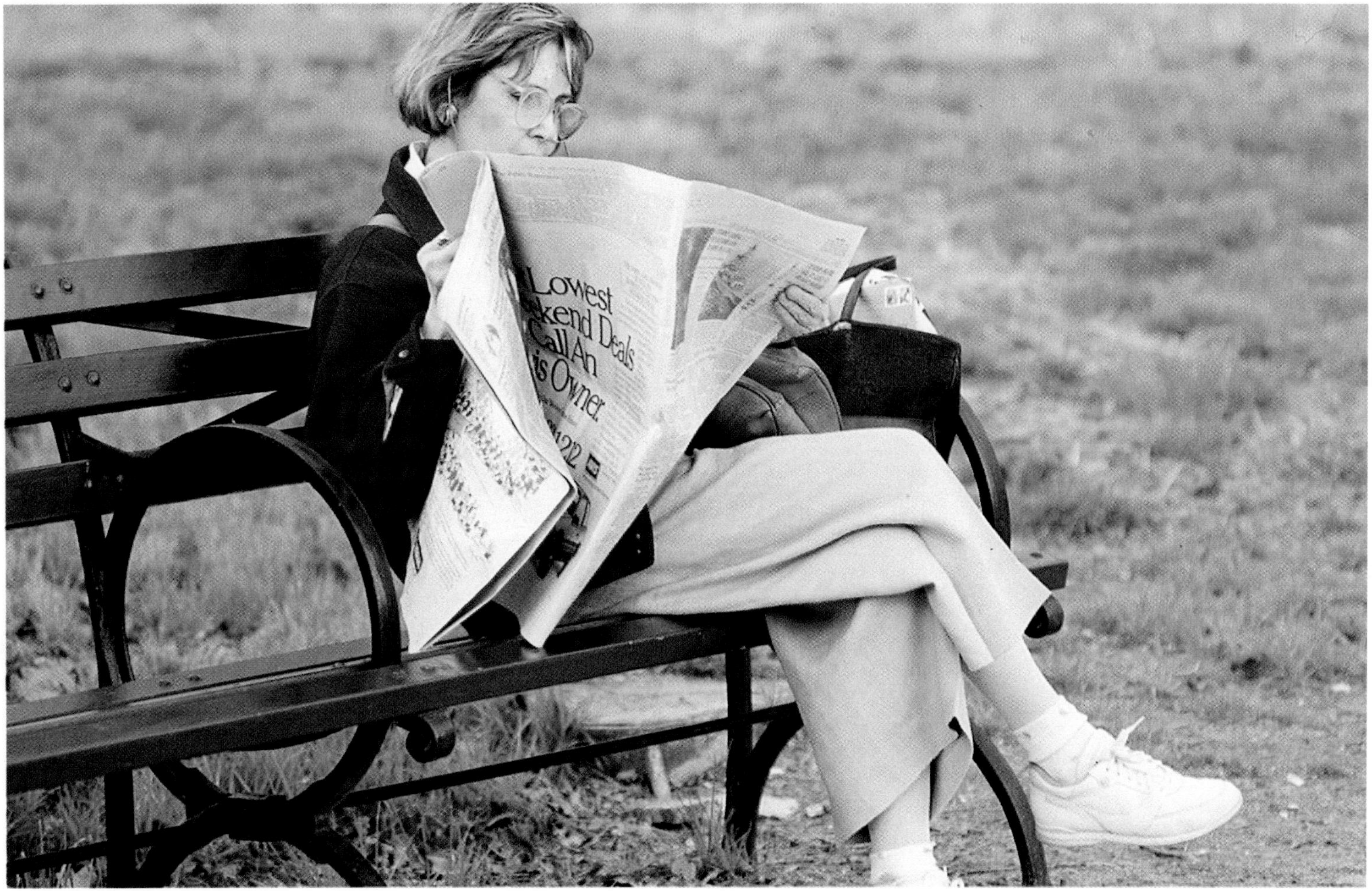

newspaper